BASE CAMP

Also by Steve Nolan:

Notes from Afghanistan

Go Deep (with NJ DeVico)

BASE CAMP

Steve Nolan

RAGGED SKY PRESS
PRINCETON, NEW JERSEY

Text and cover design by Jean Foos
All Rights Reserved
ISBN: 978-1-933974-34-7
Library of Congress Control Number: 2019953078
This book has been composed in FF Scala and Joanna MT
Printed on acid-free paper. ∞
Printed in the United States of America

Many thanks to the Pied Piper of Poetry for Bucks County, Pennsylvania, Christopher Bursk, who has been a mentor, critic, friend and cheerleader for my writing from the moment I met him. He defines the word generosity.

And to the one who blessed my life, my wife, Barbara Simmons, my Anam Cara, for her unwavering belief in me; she inspires me daily with her lifelong commitment to peace work.

Contents

Mark of Cain

Don't Refuse the Call

The Orchestration of War

The Orchestration of War

It's one of the most common souvenirs of war,
the constant ringing in the ears, or, in my case,
a high-pitched squeal presumably caused
by the Blackhawk turbine it mimics
and the artillery rounds. It's never kept me
from sleeping, thank God, but it also never
ceases to amaze how loud it is when I wake.
I go to the bathroom, I go to the kitchen,
when the house is quiet and it dominates
everything, makes me wonder how I sleep
at all with a head stuck on a note so
monotonous, so solitary, that it defies
harmony. And yet you meet others tuned
to the same pitch and for a short period
of time you can form a duo, a trio, a quartet.
At the Vet Center sometimes you form a chamber
orchestra for an hour or two a week. It helps
to have a conductor with the same note
stuck in his head but with the ability
to wield a baton better than a weapon;
the personal weapon—the most likely culprit
for the tinnitus in the first place,
how you brought on the condition with each
pull of the trigger, reminding you till the end
of your days: you were a witness, it's up to you
whether you testify.

Petrified

In Pompeii, you can walk amongst the mummies still,
charred in place, charred in motion, not
quite cremated but caught, in some cases,
mid-stride, evacuating, tending to a child.

I remember a soldier, a gunner
on an M1 tank, with over-the-horizon
targeting capability. He had problems
after the war. He said it wasn't a fair
fight. It was like shooting fish in a barrel.
When he finally came upon the enemy,
the Republican Guard, in their Soviet tanks,
they were "crispy critters," some charred
in the turret, presumably trying to escape.
He couldn't escape the results of his accuracy.
I asked him, "Would you rather it had been
the other way around?" And he gave me a look
I'd never seen before, a look that seemed
to say, "What difference does it make?"

An infantryman told me that he was hit
by an artillery round in his first battle
of Desert Storm. He lay in the sand dazed.
He looked around and saw a dismembered arm
and then a leg, and said, "What planet am I on?"

Last month I saw the picture of a five-
year-old Syrian child who survived
the massive aerial bombardment of Russian
and Syrian planes. Now he sat frozen
in the seat of an ambulance, eyes vacant.
What planet is he on? What God
rains down fire from the mouth of the volcano?

High Grounds

We must find a way
to grow something wonderful
here in these high mountains.
There have been enough
bumper crops
of poverty, disease,
hatred, and violence.

Something like coffee!
It's true what they say,
That life's simple pleasures
are the best—my cuppa joe
has me high this morning
(the caffeine jolt and the altitude)
and warms my cold hands—lovely.

Mankind needs so little, really,
a beverage to sustain you,
loved ones to comfort you,
a sunrise and a sunset to inspire you
and to time your journey—
the rest we can share;
I have it on great authority:
Jesus, the Buddha, Mohammed
and just this morning,
the supply sergeant.

IED

(Improvised Explosive Device)

A dog barks in the distance,
a dog barks in the distance—
I go to the door of my tent,
pull back the flap,
and feel the bitter winter air.
Where is this dog who wakes me
in my sleep in Afghanistan?

He won't stop shouting
to the indifferent night,
and no one responds
to his incessant cries.
This is a dog who is not loved.

If this dog were human
he would follow a strict creed.
He would make it a vocation
to inflict great suffering.
As it is, he will only bite
some unlucky one
who gets too close;
or maybe a random few.

The Battle for God

(with kudos to Karen Armstrong for her wonderful book by that title)

In 1099 the first Crusaders
felled Jerusalem and in their zeal
murdered Jews by thousands on the way.

In 1187 the Kurdish general
Saladin defeated these crusaders,
restoring Islam to Jerusalem.

In 1191 Richard the Lion-
Heart captured the port city of Acre,
near Jerusalem, and massacred
2,700 Muslims (prisoners).

In 2001, Osama Bin Laden
burned and pulverized 3,000 men,
women and children in the cities
of New York and Washington.

All thought they were doing God's bidding
and could curry favor with Him.

We sit in the foothills of the Himalayas,
in the mountains of Afghanistan,
only a few klicks from Pakistan
waiting for orders to send forth a patrol
with sniper fire, to search and destroy target.
Hoping for some up-to-date intel
on the location of Bin Laden.

Hoping for higher level intelligence
as to His whereabouts
in this battle for God.

Dreaming about a 911

Through my binoculars
I study the village of Orgune.
One can't help making comparisons
to the adobe dwellings
of our own Southwest.
All the structures
follow a fort-like pattern
with a central courtyard,
some with silo-like towers,
up to a hundred feet in height,
presumably for self-defense.
They have a somewhat medieval quality,
like little castle turrets,
and seem so out of place
in this barren, hilly landscape
but must surely bring great pride
to those who built them.

Last night a strange dream—
a Christian fundamentalist
in a stolen Piper Cub,
comes over the hilltops
and crashes deliberately
into two of the "silos"
where a group of Afghans
hold an open-air bazaar.
The locals scatter in horror
as the plane disintegrates itself
and the silos in a mini fireball.
The Afghan people stare in disbelief
as I try desperately
to explain that none of this
has anything to do
with Jesus Christ.

Anima

("No greater love than this..." —for Jose Pantoja, army medic)

You have no idea how many ways
the word "fuck" can be used until you come
to a combat zone. It's a verb, it's a noun,
it's an adjective. It's release!
Here one can almost feel the clash of horns,
the rutting elk, or see the puffed out
peacock feathers that seduce the hen;
the flexed-muscle tattoo images—
the stained glass windows to a man's soul.

Today I will medevac a soldier who
caught a bullet in the temple and,
without it penetrating any bone,
went sub-Q-round-the-skull and
out the back of his head—the lucky bastard!

And I will sit and talk with yet another,
a medic, who has earned two purple hearts,
who wears a three-inch scar across his cheek
where a bullet grazed him while he worked
to save a fallen friend. This badge of courage,
destined to give "street-cred" once he's home.

What goes unsung: the exorcism of
that inner rib which birthed a heart of gold,
that knelt beside his buddies, nine in all
(with shrapnel flying, here, then there)
and ministered their wounds amidst a fire-
fight. That same heart which won't allow
this medic to take a free ride home
and leave his "guys" without their "doc."

There is a rite of passage very rarely
understood: when all is said,
the wounded one becomes the Savior.

The Fog of War

There will be no flight today.
We are waiting for the fog to clear.
In truth, it's not fog but a heavy snow,
surrounding the white mountains,
like a dense cloud cover.
We were supposed to go to Tillman today,
a forward operating base on the
Afghan/Pakistan border;
named after Pat Tillman, the
Arizona Cardinal who gave up
pro football at-the-drop-of
two towers in New York City.
He became a soldier on the front
lines of a war on terror.
Of course, war *is* terror—
five percent terror and ninety-five percent boredom,
but what a hellish five percent,
chasing elusive ghosts in these hills,
ghosts we once armed against the
Soviets—our payback for them
arming North Vietnam.

If something can go wrong it will.
That is what we call "the fog of war";
miscalculations with rockets, mortars,
even "friendly fire." When you kill
a "friendly," you've killed your own.
I'm told that's what happened to Pat Tillman.
How many millionaires go to war
as Army Rangers? I've never heard of it
before. How many athletes leave the game
they love, to reach for patriotic duty?

So we named this camp in his honor;
Camp Tillman, where he is

watching us upon that distant hill.
We were hoping for clear skies
and all systems go, but now we
have to "hurry up and wait," a way
of life you must get used to—

and we are
still waiting for the fog
to clear.

From Arlington My Father Visits Me

I saw a yellow host rise above
a purple mountain altar just this morn.
I see a tincture of the blood of Christ
in every snow-melt mountain stream.
And in each mud-n-brick abode—poverty;
dirt floors, animals and humans
living in proximity.

Last night, a star so bright
I had to wonder were there any
wise men left to follow.

And in my dreams I joined a ground assault
to flush out enemy combatants
from a village late at night...

...We went from house to house
fully locked and loaded, breaking
wooden doors and mangers down.
Repeatedly surprised, this is what we found:
my father, in every humble dwelling,
huddled with each family on bended knee
reciting his beloved rosary.

Old Farts in a Young War

When younger soldiers talk of sex,
they jest.
When one of us chimes in,
they listen;
pretty much the same routine
if someone wants to talk religion.

They look upon our wrinkled skin
and graying hair, and monitor
how much weight we put upon a bar;
and can't believe we're always
looking for a patch of shade
to lounge in folding canvas chairs
to "shoot-the-shit"
and chomp cigars.

They like to call us "old farts"
when we take-a-load-off;
and they joke our panatelas
are firmer than our members.
They show us pictures
of their nubile nymphs and say:
"Take a good look what you're missin', Doc,
cause you couldn't handle her
even with Viagra."
But we know
it's our approval
that they're after.

All in all, they're glad they're young
and think it just a nightmare
to be atop, or, God forbid,
over the proverbial hill.

Youth always thinks it has the upper
hand because they're toned and firm;

and we are, for the most part,
soft and pudgy.

But it is always an advantage
being old, because, you see,
we already had our chance to be their age
but they will only get to be ours
if they're lucky.

Staring at the Stars—a Revelation

I awoke and heard a voice
like thunder coming from the mortar pit.
I beheld the moon, as if it were seated on
a white horse cloud, with streaming mane
and tail draped over the mountains.

The mortar fired another round over
the jagged ridge—a great sword
hurled through the heavens.
The moon slipped behind cloud cover
turning my white celestial steed
to sackcloth and then to black.

I thought of all the warriors hidden in caves
over the border waiting to avenge
some blood, or imagined blood
spilt in some crusade.

At the same time: my own soldiers
on the ridge-top with NVGs
searched for pale robes moving in
the shadows of a valley of death;
searched as long as it took
until the killing was completed.

Shooting stars punctuated the night
like tracers; so many stars
falling to earth and consumed before
they hit the ground—like ripe figs
hanging low in a garden.

And every nervous soldier
crouched all night long,
waiting for the night sky to recede,
its giant scroll rolled up—
rolling with it all the nightmares,

of a black sun and a moon
that's turned to blood. Rolling up night
itself, so that with the birth of light
every soldier, every commander,
every rich man and every king
could put down their arms,
come down from the mountains
and walk on water.

Man in the Language of God

(on the way home from Salerno, Afghanistan)

One soldier
        can't wait to see his girlfriend.
One soldier
        can't wait to see his eight-month-old son.
One soldier
        displays a nude "goddess" on his laptop.
Then
        a commotion at the doorway
        as one soldier tries killing a large spider
        with "tough-actin" Tinactin foot spray.

Most sleep the day away—
exhausted young men
dreaming of home...
Michigan and Ohio
and other such places,
with Indian names,
the history of which
they know as little
as that of the Taliban.

Band of Brothers

I loved them.

I did not love them beforehand—
in honky-tonk bars drunk with alcohol,
football, and crude jokes about women,
including the women standing close by.
The ones who they wanted desperately
to undress (except for the one with the flattest chest
or bad teeth or too much adipose tissue).

And I would not love them after, with their fears
of socialism stoked by rich radio
pundits they believed shared a common
patriotism; not when they maligned
their Commander in Chief with a level of venom
never uttered at anyone white. Not when
they purchased weapons, sported Confederate flags
and feared big government would torch their Second
Amendment church if they stood idly by.

But there in those mountains when they mounted up
for a ground assault convoy with a mission-first
acceptance of daily life and no discernible
trace of fear; or at midnight, when I heard
a chopper coming in with casualties and they
insisted their buddies be seen first no matter
what their own wounds—there in the medical aid
station where it was clear to see that they
were all good thieves on a cross, or when we hunkered-
down in the same bomb shelter taking incoming,
I wrote it in my journal, I said it out loud
drowned by the noise of a Blackhawk,
I thought it repeatedly when alone sipping
coffee in an observation post:

I loved them.

The Martyr, the Engineer

They show me to his room,
the Taliban leader called "The Engineer"
(due to his expertise with IEDs).
He's in ICU room thirteen—interesting.
His luck has definitely run out.
I think of an old expression: "One man's
terrorist is another man's freedom fighter."
The martyr or the engineer?

Has he earned a free ticket to heaven?
Or did he put himself on a sure road to hell?
The surgeons removed his spleen,
his left arm, and sundry parts in March,
following a firefight with Afghan Army forces
down range. I was there
the night they brought him in.
It is two months later. I am his only visitor—
maybe his last visitor. He is sleeping now.

At least in dreams, does he get reprieve
from his pain? He will soon
have an answer to all the questions
of which he's never had any doubts.

Will he sit in paradise surrounded by virgins?
Or will he simply lie somewhere
in the soil of Afghanistan,
with numerous worms crawling in and out?
Or, perhaps, Lucifer needs another freedom fighter
in his age-old war of allegiance
against those angels, who, to this day,
still occupy his original homeland.

The Call to Prayer in the Village of Lwara

The magpie perched above the mosque,
on the highest branch of the tamarack tree,
is neither mocking God nor custom!
His view of life in this valley is sharp
and clear from his high vantage point.

His presence is not known to the men inside
who are adjusting prayer rugs and whose fingers
fumble with their beads; nor is
his presence known to my fellow soldiers
in the observation post that overlooks
the village of Lwara and whose fingers
fumble with the wires attached to mines.

The smaller birds, resembling sparrows
(but with darker heads), look like hooded nuns
and sit vigil on the concertina wire,
studying the valley's simple palette
of colors: the pearl-gray snow, the
winding coffee river's rocky shoals,
the bright-green plots of winter wheat
terraced down the long, brown slopes
of these barren, yet majestic hills.

The magpie has rested but a very
few feet above the loudspeaker
(a staple of every local mosque)
mounted at the apex of this simple,
tin-roofed place of common worship
(built by the United States Army
at the urgent request of tribal leaders).

I worry that this bird will soon be
blasted from his slender pulpit as
we approach the time for evening prayer.

Of course, our mortars could go off
at any moment, scattering all
the birds along the mountain's eastern ridge.

He looks so pious on his pinnacle
observing village life and at times
joining the variety of song
rising from the nests throughout the glen.

At four o'clock he's flushed abruptly from
his choir loft by the loud and somewhat plaintive
cry of *Allahu Akbar* (God Is Great).
I can hear the village men reciting
from the Koran as I retrieve my pocket Bible
and start to read my own daily prayer.

The magpie has sailed across the valley
to the top of yet another tamarack
tree—his place of worship, where, in Spring,
(because God in-deed is truly great)
leaves will flutter like the pages of
a sacred manuscript.

The Water Bearers

There is so little color in this valley.
Lwara has many hues of brown,
from peaks to lowest wadi. The women
in their shades of red or purple pop out
of the landscape like opium blossoms. This
morning I watched three such flowers
make their way down the slopes from
their village compound, a half a mile
to the riverbed, to fill their vessels and
strike out again with silver pots
balanced on their heads. To find life
or color in this land, you must find water.
Men in their dark clothes of black
or brown or navy blue busily patch
dwellings where al Qaeda rockets blasted
through, creating total disrepair.
The women silently descend the hill;
make a second trek; for liquid sustains
the clan and helps the men coagulate
cement. Mornings, women tend their crops,
hurl rocks at wayward goats
who've gotten free and breached the winter wheat.
And in the afternoon the women stray
into the hills, and come back with wood
in giant bundles hoisted, once again,
atop their head. Evening sees men
to the mosque, all work has stopped
by prayer time, and in this abode, most humble,
all can dream of golden domes or minarets.
For centuries men have had the duty
of constructing temples, mosques and monuments:
The Great Buddhas in Bamiyan Province—
recently destroyed by Taliban.
Women, as they have for centuries,

tap the rivers for their life force,
so that all can bathe and eat and drink.

A critic once told Samuel Clemens that
his writings were certainly no classics.
Twain agreed, and further stated that
to read a classic was like drinking fine wine,
whereas, his work, more like water.
But everyone needs water.

Oppenheimer on a Train

(The Cottonwoods)

At Los Alamos soldiers hunkered
down in trenches, put on goggles to
protect their eyes from the flash. When
the mushroom rose above the cotton-
woods, Oppenheimer later wrote,
"I remembered the line from the Hindu
scripture, the Bhagavad-Gita.
Vishnu is trying to persuade the prince
that he should do his duty, and, to
impress him, takes on his multi-
armed form and says, 'NOW I
AM BECOME DEATH, the destroyer of worlds.'"

My mother likes to tell the story
of how she was traveling with me when
I was young and met Oppenheimer
on a train. She says he was quite
taken with me and had kind words
about my looks, my curiosity.
I don't know what to make of that now.
Perhaps he was radioactive.
Perhaps he touched me.
Perhaps there was a blessing he bestowed
upon me, like Vishnu, that I
would grow to be a man of duty, or
perhaps, he would have hoped,
a planter of cottonwoods.

(Los Alamos: Spanish, meaning "The Cottonwoods")

Let the Children Come to Me

All week there'd been commotion at the clinic,
an unexpected appendectomy,
a one-year-old burned by
an exploding kitchen stove, the Afghan soldier
who discharged his weapon, accidentally
shooting himself through the shoulder, the
little boy with the spiral-fractured femur,
and the old man's severely lacerated leg—
a nasty-looking wound, now infected.

It was early morning and I was sleepy,
needing a cup of coffee, as I stomped
the snow from my boots and stepped through
the entryway to the Medical Aid Station.

Sitting on one end of a raised litter
was a middle-aged man with rust-colored
skin and loosely fitting Afghan attire;
beside him, sat a little girl. His
daughter? Rarely did parents bring
their own children to the clinic, a mystery
we were trying to solve. Was this her uncle,
grandfather, or just a neighbor? On a
nearby table, the girl's older brother
was treated for a separated shoulder.

She turned her head toward me, her eyes
brightened, and the broadest smile of joy
spread across her face. I was surprised,
but flattered—surprised because so few
Afghan people smiled at me in greeting
(and never had it happened in the clinic),
flattered that she chose to smile at "me."
I almost turned around to see if there
was someone at my stern, but

the door had closed behind and I could
feel it pressing on my rucksack.

Her smile was like a smile of recognition
that one reserves for close relatives
or special friends. I smiled back and she
seemed to take delight in this—smiling
even wider and more radiantly
than before, which I would not have thought
possible. My own smile grew.

I looked at the man next to her, he was
perhaps my own age—fifty-something.
He was weather-beaten and his eyes were dull.
He looked at me with neither anger nor
disgust, neither joy nor sorrow,
a detachment that one only feels when
cultures clash so plainly, language can't
be bridged. Finding no warmth there,
I looked again at the little girl and saw
nothing but interest—no, on second thought,
interest would be the wrong word, because
there was no gulf between us in which
to cast the hook of interest. There was
a smile, a mimicked nod, a playful glance.

Why this child was capable of
transcending age and gender, I know not.
How she saw past nationality,
ethnic features, or religious creed,
I cannot say. But of this I'm certain:
if man could plumb the reaches
of the thoughts which sparked that smile,
there would never be a need for war.

Even the Dalai Lama Wears Glasses

"I am America"

I have multiple myeloma.
There is no cure.
There is no known cause.
There are theories:
overexposure to benzene,
overexposure to chlorine.
I can't help wondering
a hundred different things:
the lead paint I ate as a child,
the asbestos tiles that flaked down
on me in fourth grade,
the DDT I consumed with my fruit,
the other pesticides I used
on the lawn and garden,
my genetically modified soy and corn,
my tainted milk,
my poisoned beef,
the mercury in my seafood,
the "new car smell,"
the "new carpet smell,"
the auto emissions,
the microwave radiation,
my excessive cell phone use,

the depleted uranium
I was exposed to in Iraq,
my proximity to the burn pits
in Afghanistan,
my living so close to the Love Canal,
my cleanup efforts at Three Mile Island,
my total awe at the flash
and mushroom cloud at Los Alamos,
before I was born,
before you were born,
before every one of us was born
into the brave new world.

Bucket List

You'd think if you had less time to live
you would not waste time
but you do (with the best of them).
You spend a long time petting the cat.
You clean hair out of a drain
that could go unclogged for months.
You contemplate getting on a ladder
to do the gutters for no apparent reason
other than not particularly wanting to pay bills.

You do the same with driving, shopping;
if anything you waste *more* time
simply because you are more aware of it
as a commodity *you* can control.
You've heard all about this bucket list
but you'd have to run off
and abandon your friends and loved ones
right at the point where they've
become the most interesting,
when you see more in their eyes,
hear more nonsense come from their brains,
feel such truth come from their hearts,
that you could fill a bucket.

You Can't Take It with You

I have been ill now nine months,
the same time it takes to birth a child,
and I wonder just what it is I've grown
in that time—just what it is I'm
supposed to give birth to.

My parents always said, "You can't take it
with you," which seemed to be a message
about attachment and the ability to
discriminate that which matters from
the mere collection of things. I saw a movie
this week, *Straight Outta Compton*, about
a few young African American men
who came out of poverty, and fell victim
to their own excess. I heard another
story this week about a white boy
from privilege who escaped from a home
of abuse by taking public transportation
from the suburbs to the city to roam
the art museums, the Franklin Institute,
and cherish those valued objects, those
peaceful hours. He grew his talent, his skills,
his moxie enough to own a home
that became a museum of its own, filled
with rare and beautiful possessions that
will have to be archived someday.

My parents also said, "Count your blessings"—
so this morning I wake early, way before
the sun, gently kiss my wife and roll out
of bed in search of coffee. The house is quiet.
Even the dog does not stir, does not
want to join me on my Starbucks run.
I grab my clothes and dress in the kitchen
before slipping quietly out the back

door. I hold in my hands the few possessions
I need so as not to be naked in the world.
I pull on my shoes, my socks, my pants, my shirt,
my belt, and step out into the darkness,
lift my head toward heaven and see
Orion's Belt, realize the only thing
we ever really have to show is light
against the darkness; even I can see
the Big Dipper is empty.

Go Deep

He draws a diagram of an iceberg.
The tip floating above the waves,
the massive body below menacing
by its sheer presence. He is a healer,
he does not want me to think
it's such clear sailing by what I can see
with the numbers. He wants me to go
deep, do the heavy-duty chemo,
get more of the iceberg than what's
possible with the treatment regimens
we've tried so far. My numbers
are climbing again after six months
on the decline. "Go deep"—it's
the best chance for long-term remission,
though there is no cure, we know we can't
get all the iceberg and there are
only so-many lifeboats at our
disposal, only so-many parties
left in the grand ballroom before
we all see a watery death. After
my bone biopsy I need a drink, a little
entertainment—so we accept
an invitation to meet neighbors at
the Temperance House, temperance the
one thing not in large supply
inside. There is music, there is laughter,
there is flirting, there is a celebration
of life everywhere; a wonderful
anesthesia for all the hidden
dangers of life. It feels as if I've joined
a great party, late at night, below deck.
But I feel more like the captain who
can never fully join any party,
especially when his duty is to get
back to the bridge—so he can be the first
to witness the obscure shape on the horizon.

Trading Places

The homeless man asks to change seats with me.
Apparently he sits in the same chair every day.
There is a strange comfort in routine—rich or poor.
I wonder if he ever thinks of truly changing places
with the patrons of the coffee shop.
He looks like he has had a hard life,
but I doubt if he would want my cancer
even if he could erase the memories of his childhood.

He resembles a Vietnam vet I met years ago
who suffered from two wars—
the first, living in a trailer with his tormentor,
his mother's boyfriend,
who threw him against a wall
the first time they were left alone
and simply said with a smile,
"I can't wait to marry your mother
so I get to do this every day."

I'll take the cancer,
a foe for which I have a fighting chance.

Angela Merkel's Comb

Did you think you would stay young?
You did, didn't you?
You weren't totally crazy!
You actually expected the first gray hair,
the first wrinkle, the first belly fat—
just not that soon. You knew you would
get old eventually but you just knew
that you would be one of the few who
would do it gracefully. My brother once
told me he saw a study where they asked
people if they didn't know their chronological
age, how old did they feel inside?
The most common answer was twenty-five.
These were middle-aged people. Middle
age is not the problem—you can manage
that awkwardly but acceptably
with a little help from the health club,
the garment industry, the cosmetic manufacturer,
the pharmaceuticals. It's old age
that's the problem. You don't want to go there
because then you're seriously going to have
to think about death—the end of everything
you know, and, either the end, period, or
possibly the beginning of the best
damned time you ever had. But the
creators of that scenario
had to go and make it like Vegas,
a gamble, with God and the devil proprietors
of different hotels. It's hard enough facing
loss of personal power, personal mobility,
did they have to add uncertainty
to the formula? Don't you just hate
nature films about salmon spawning?
Their mighty struggle upstream all
the way? And all the way losing calcium,

becoming deformed? To leave their shot at
progeny and then, curtains! Don't you secretly
love all the birthing films—with the young
slimy ones taking their first steps
into the world, discovering everything?

You expected the arthritis, you were at least
semi-prepared; but not the cancer. You never
saw yourself in a chemo lab any more
than you saw yourself in a wheelchair
in a nursing home. My favorite bumper sticker
was always: SHIT HAPPENS, but after studying
eloquent philosophers, I never knew
why. Intuitively we know there is
no remission against the storms that brew
on this planet. It doesn't always happen
to the other guy. You never thought you'd be
divorced. You never thought you'd lose a child.
You never thought you'd leave your professorship
in Prague and be herded like cattle to Theresienstadt;
never thought you'd leave Aleppo for
a leaky boat and cry in front of strangers
who rescued you, and gave you water—weep
uncontrollably when one of them
offered you a comb.

Jaywalking

Since the diagnosis I've started jaywalking a lot. What the hell do I care? They've given me a death sentence and with that there's no time for trivial rules. I envision some cop calling me over for a lecture on public safety and how he's really doing it for my own good. I remember when I returned from Afghanistan and I got stopped for jaywalking, the authority figure in my face but politely telling me to use the crosswalk for my own protection—a week after being rocketed by Taliban. I got a lot of speeding tickets back then, not so much from being reckless, as being spaced out, or ignoring the really stupid laws. Rules are rules, we can't afford to take into account the reasons a person might break them. This morning I listened to a presidential candidate who said we want legal immigrants, not illegal.

I went for my morning coffee, jaywalking across the busiest intersection in town, and reminisced about one speeding ticket I didn't get. While barreling across an Indian reservation at 20 mph over the posted speed, I got pulled over by the Reservation Police. The Native American cop started to write my ticket until he spotted my ACU (Army Combat Uniform) in the back of my car. He asked me, "You been to Iraq?" I answered, "Afghanistan, just back." He stopped writing the ticket, pointed to himself and said, "Vietnam. Do me a favor, brother, and don't speed on my reservation, okay? We've got panthers that cross here." I thanked him. I could see he knew exactly why I was speeding. And I know exactly why he has to live on a reservation. I know exactly what happens when people get scared or greedy. I know exactly whether Christopher Columbus was a legal or illegal immigrant.

Random

My disease is random, I guess; the experts
have no known cause. It was the ping-
pong ball with the number floating in the air-
wash at the lottery pick—except those
are the winning numbers (my blood work
not so much). It has been exactly
one year since my diagnosis;
one year of many random things—
earthquakes, floods, mass exodus
from war, from deprivation, from brutality.
I'm not saying the perpetrators were random—
those that committed vicious acts
like the mass beheadings on a beach
that they filmed for the world; but the victims
were random—wrong place, wrong time,
wrong religion. Or maybe nothing is random.

Maybe there is a fantastic computer out there
that runs the universe precisely and we will
see someday how it all makes perfect sense.
Or perhaps God is behind it all, even
the bad things, like the story of the first
thing to go viral or mutate, an angel named
Lucifer, who was given certain powers,
certain dominion over bad things—
his areas of responsibility are
rather vague, but cancer would be his kind
of thing, another thing to gamble over
with the Lord to test someone's mettle
like the famous story of Job. I hate
that story! It shows a stupid God,
a poor leader, getting sucked into a wager
with one of his former lieutenants; and the moral
would have to be that nothing in life is truly
random, but a calculated bet, like the dollar

you throw down for the lottery ticket expecting
to lose. I can't think of my life that way
unless everything good was also random;
every smile, every laugh, every
tear dried by a loving hand or kiss,
every embrace of a child or grandchild
or lover, or, in my case, the discovery
of my one true love near the end of my life
so that, random or not, I finally
won the lottery.

Still Life

(for NJ)

You told me your news.
We went for a walk in the park.
You showed me the place
you wanted your ashes spread.
We heard a bullfrog down by the creek
calling a mate or something equally urgent.
We sucked honeysuckle.
You said, "Don't tell Barb but I love you."
I said, "Don't tell Glenn but I love you too."
We had our, what's becoming routine,
talk about the purpose of life,
whether God is a fairy tale;
tried to cover all the angles—
settled for: God is love.

We went back to the house.
You showed me your latest painting.
I read poetry.
You chased a squirrel away from the bird feeder.
There was a palette of color there—
a cardinal, a blue jay, a yellow finch.
I brought you the first strawberries from the garden.
We admired them for a moment.
Then we did what begged to be done.
They were very ripe.
They were sweet on the tongue.
There was no time to paint them.

Visiting My Sister's Grave with Cancer

It's not quite grammatically correct.
It sounds as if the grave has cancer.
And many of them do
along with MS, diabetes, stroke, heart disease—
that's what took you,
a rare abnormality of the heart
at five months of age.
Months-of-age is grammatically correct.
Who makes up these rules we all live by?
I know who makes the rule we all die by.
The cemetery is named after his mother.
Do I have to capitalize the word His?
Is it a tiny sin to keep it lowercase?
I'm not interested in a God
who gives a goddamn about such things.
He didn't give a God-damn to save you,
and my situation is still in question.

I was four years old at your passing
and I don't have a single memory of you.
So why do I stand here crying?
Why do I bother talking to the dead?
Why do I feel I will be joining you at long last?
Is it too late to be a big brother?
Can you even be a big brother to an angel
or a ghost or whatever it is we become?
Are you even here in row eleven,
plot nineteen, grave four? Or do you
come back whenever there is a visitor?
Like a heavenly rule grants you parole,
or a day-pass for special occasions.

I feel you here,
you whom I've never known,
you who were never educated,

romanced, married, bore children,
all the things we deem important
in building character, resumés, legacy;
all the things for a eulogy—
the eulogy you never had,
just a silent funeral with a father in shock,
a mother barely in motion,
and a little boy in a state of amnesia.
I have a feeling that the list of earthly accomplishments
has little meaning where you are,
that to be an angel also requires amnesia
to the long list of opposites
starting with the knowledge of good and evil.
Not the elucidated knowledge of theologians
but the simple playground type:
Good = little sister
Evil = the bully who pushed her into the ditch.

I always fought bullies!
You would have had your avenger,
but I guess you know that.
I have a feeling you know my entire resumé.
I tried to bring home good-enough grades
because your report card was always blank.

Or maybe I have everything backwards.
Maybe you were the one always protecting me—
until I finally came up against the one bully
you couldn't beat—like your heart valves—
that even God Almighty
couldn't find the time to change.

If you're not *as* busy maybe you could
do something about my bloodwork;
or make a big brother proud,
open an oven door
and slowly pull six million cells
back into the marrow of humanity.

Democracy

I got the results of the MRI—
torn labrum both hips.
I had to Google it—the labrum
is a ring of cartilage that follows the outside rim
of the socket of your hip joint. The labrum
acts like a rubber seal or gasket to help
hold the ball at the top of your thighbone
securely within your hip socket. So I've
finally blown a gasket—a prediction of many
for years. "Running is rough on the joints"
a deceased roadrunner buddy of mine,
Syl Ludington, used to say. "It's rough
on the joints I used to frequent before I took
up running," Syl was a jokester of the first order
and a devout Catholic like my father,
an usher, a minister of the Eucharist, liked
to go to Mass every day—the church
itself a labrum, a protection, a seal
that was never broken, never torn for him
or my father as it was for me the day
I was expelled from Catholic school. That was
a great birthing—after the initial shock,
the slap on the rear, the peeing on the doctor
(as my mother said I did during my physical birth)—
called agnosticism. I discovered
those other births, Judaism,
Buddhism, Hinduism, Islam;
just as I discovered others talking
in tongues—German, Spanish, Italian and French,
and never would have thought English the true
mother tongue of all, or America
the mother nation of them all, even though
she took in so many orphans. Labrum
in Latin means lip or lip-like
part—coming from the Latin, Labium.

Labia is the plural noun, the folds
of skin bordering the vulva, the end
of the birth canal—the doorway into the new
world, as my mother birthed me, Holy
Mother the Church birthed me, the Maiden
in the Harbor (with her torch held aloft
like the bright lights of the birthing room), birthed
so many, saying, once you have breached
this threshold, there is no going back.

I'm Leaning toward the Milky Way

My friend who needs an organ transplant
talks about the highs and lows
of each possible donor,
where he sits on the wait list, how
his deteriorating health made him
a less viable candidate, how
he may move up the list soon
due to his recently improved numbers.

His wife brings him a small meal and then
asks if he would like something sweet—
tapioca pudding, strawberry
rhubarb or a Milky Way candy bar?
I'm leaning toward the Milky Way,
he says and she tracks down a Halloween-
size miniature chocolate
and unwraps it for him.

We talk about foreign travels, current
events, the state of the world. The President
sang "Amazing Grace" this week
and we marvel that music and illness are doors
to the spiritual—illness starting
the day humans left the Garden of Eden,
nostalgia for a celestial home dominating
our thoughts ever since; think of flight,
think of rocketry, think of satellites
and space stations. We sent a probe to Mars
but we did not find heaven;
not a cherub or harp has yet
appeared on NASA or SOYUZ cameras.
Perhaps farther out in the solar system,
farther out in some magnificent,
luminous galaxy we will find
those pearly gates—I'm leaning toward
the Milky Way and the one woman's hand
offering it, saying, this may not
be Paradise, but this is love.

Perfect

Sixty-three years old and on my honeymoon:
the travel smooth,
the village quaint,
the old inn cozy,
the food and drink exquisite.
The king-size bed almost adequate
for our intentions.
My bride so beautiful clothed
and unclothed.
The way we express our love—
every cell of the body, every
part of the soul is nurtured.
Then the laughter we share
before going to sleep.
Everything was perfect
like the day they said I had cancer
and the whole world stopped
so I could look at it.

Even the Dalai Lama Wears Glasses

"The conceit of a long, lucky life is that
bad things happen to others," is how
Tom Brokaw describes the news of his
cancer. I too, had a long lucky life.
I was used to winning and turning the occasional loss
into victory. I was respectful of science
but also a believer in prayers, in miracles,
and in the old adage, "God helps those who help
themselves." A favorite joke of mine for years
was of a minister whose car breaks down
in the country. He walks to a farm for help
and proceeds to praise the crops, the livestock,
the barn, the house, and keeps telling the farmer
"You must thank God every day
for such blessings." Finally, the farmer has heard
enough and responds, "Yes, Reverend, I do,
but you should have seen this place when He
had it all to Himself." With cancer, friends
and loved ones comb the web and offer
myriad forms of advice, helpful hints,
the latest research. It's a bit overwhelming
and runs the gamut from latest clinical trials
to miracle cures. Perhaps it's also conceit
to think if you were unlucky enough
to get sick, you might be lucky enough
to get well—it's simple mathematical
law of averages or nature's balance.
You hear the power of mind, spirit, prayer,
meditation, guided imagery, has worked
for some and you would like to be in that
number when those saints go marching in
to remission. You might even think you deserve
to be in that number due to past virtues
but then you remember Christ on the cross,
Joan of Arc on the funeral pyre, Bobby

Kennedy, Martin Luther King Jr.
cut down in their prime and their virtues
seem to make yours pale. Someone
sent me a video of Wayne Dyer
and he talks about spiritual surgery.
That gave me hope and then he suddenly
died. Bad timing! Or not. My doctor
in his white lab coat is starting to look
much more like a shaman these days.
I see that he's a healer and really cares.
Surrender is a difficult path to tread.
Fighting is my natural stance. I'm
a well-balanced Irishman—a chip
on both shoulders—but never blind;
always mindful that you can never have
too much vision, that you can't
do everything alone. Even
the Dalai Lama was helped by the CIA
when he fled to India, even the Dalai Lama
wears glasses.

Last Night at the Widow's Poetry Reading
on Martha's Vineyard

I took my wife.
It was not her crowd
but, due to my illness, will be.
It was honest, it was heartfelt,
it was earthy, practical. They discussed
the obvious: the loneliness, the void
to be filled by one when the living space was two—
the awkwardness of friends, the incessant, "How
are you doing?" to be answered a thousand ways:
gut-wrenching, honest, sarcastic, humorous,
depending on the mood. There were surprisingly
few references to religion, the afterlife.
The focus was on this life and the struggle
between a healthy new start and the
shrine one tends to preserve for someone
who made a shrine of your own heart; what
to do with the cufflinks, shoes and ties—
are they treasures for those who loved or
grim reminders of the deceased? There is
a need to display photographs and special
gifts, the bizarre tug-of-war between
storage and staging so as not to offend
the dead but not to discourage the new lover.
The realization that no one is replaceable.
You don't get over love—you put it in
its own special drawer so that it can be
hidden when it needs to be—retrieved
at times when we need to be reminded,
why the heart has chambers.

Harvesting in Spring

In the background Loreena McKennitt sings
"I can see the light in the distance,"
while my wife weeds and plants in the garden.
Winter is finally over and celebration
is everywhere, bursting mostly from warm
earth, but birds are early morning worshippers.

The tulips are tall and announce the word: "Spring"
on their lips in a whisper, really; their stems
must have cells of steel to erect from frozen
ground with the determination to scrape sky.
I need some of that determination
to outgrow a cancer that wants to take
over the garden. The oncologists
have used various forms of pesticide
to help with the weeding but I wish we could
employ my wife's painstaking methods
of making room for beauty. A new season
has arrived along with a new course of treatment.

I will be in and out of the hospital
by May. They will have plucked the magical bulbs
needed; stored them in a freezer even
colder than winter soil—each and every
one programmed for resurrection after
they, apologetically, hang me on a cross.

My wife and I make love more frequently
lately. Yesterday she lifted her wine
glass to toast me, us, many more Aprils.
We got the phone call just the other day—
the insurance company has approved everything!
It's an omen, I tell her, you always want
your stem cells harvested in Spring.

Mark of Cain

Psalm 139

(the question of worthiness)

And if I made my bed in hell, You are there, too.
You tricked me. I could think of no place farther
away to run. Why do I go to the tavern
and cast my line without a lead, let my hook,
my bait, float on the surface for the minnows
to nibble, rather than let it sink to the depths?
Why do I refuse to discard the cracked
mirror, invite seven more years
bad luck, seven years of distorting
Your countenance—refuse to accept
that Your image and likeness could be me?
Perhaps I don't want to see You so small,
reduced to a phrase we might call self-love.
Must I be an old man before
I stop spinning this tragic love story—
this yearning for the One who got away?

If I ascended to heaven, there You are
telling Moses and Peter to open the gate
for Your most fickle lover, telling Solomon
not to give me a tour of the kingdom,
telling Magdalene not to wash the road
from my feet, and that, I will not be shocked
to find, You want to do that personally.

Crucifixion

Luwanda lives on the ground floor.
She wears pajamas that bear the print
of a *New York Times* comforter—grimy
like the windows, like the brick itself
in her welfare hotel on 42nd Street.
She watches like a cat
the raving prostitutes,
the silent junkies.
She is three and hugs the shadows,
the small places,
the safe spaces in the halls
at night
on a scatter of cigarette butts.
Luwanda sleeps
when the neighborhood sleeps,
at 2:00 or 3:00,
and will go to school
when the time comes,
take tests manufactured in Minnesota
that never ask questions
about old men in elevators
who did dirties,
did dirties
to Luwanda
when she was three.
Agnus Dei, qui tollis peccata mundi.
The lamb of God is paying the price
of the human condition.

Billy Graham in China

Mao's four-story statue came toppling down
following the visit of Billy Graham,
that great windblown overcoat sailing
after the famous hand raised in greeting.
Workers severed the Great Helmsman
under cover of darkness,
leaving an empty pedestal.

The sanctum of Chinese Communism
opened its doors to the evangelist
(the Prime Minister's welcoming committee,
university students in Beijing).
They asked him why he believed in God
(those who had once carried
the *Little Red Book*
during the Cult of Personality).

And those who could still remember
the Great Leap Forward
stepped into the large dent on the pavement—
curious as Delilah.

The President in Selma

It passed quietly,
the anniversary of Bloody Sunday,
although the president of the United States
made a trip and walked the bridge
with some of the original heroes.
There was a flatness to the coverage,
as if Ferguson had tired us of the issue,
and ISIS had erased memories of the Ku Klux Klan;
and the economic hardships of Americans
took precedence over past sins—
as if a black man in the White House
put a cherry on a sundae
that anyone could order at a lunch counter
and we could all wash our hands
in a common restroom.

Will Be Done

Johnny Z awaited execution.
We have a time-honored gift
of retribution for the family
of the victim. Johnny had always
maintained his innocence, but who
doesn't? There were experts
who testified as to mental impairment;
other experts saying he never got
a fair trial, a competent defense,
an unbiased jury—the things we can't
spend too much time worrying about.
Not with murder! Not with starving
children in the world, relatives
dying of incurable disease. We
simply get overwhelmed with the number
of problems we've got to solve. Now
they even talk of a meteor that will come
close to the earth and would end all life
on the planet, but the scientists tell us
it will miss and we trust them.
We trust jury selection, law schools,
judgeships, the cop walking the beat,
the jailor. The executioner will do our will.
Not every prisoner is John the Baptist
screaming prophetic things from his cell.
The chaplain was turned away;
and the corrections officer turns the key
to unlock the door. He's come to escort
Johnny and Johnny whispers:
"You can't fool me, God,
I recognize You even in disguise."

Mark of Cain

The killings.
You know the ones I'm talking about.
The ones in Israel, Syria, Libya,
Yemen, Afghanistan; in Ukraine,
Nigeria, Mexico, Iraq.
The ones involving human trafficking,
drug cartels, militias, makeshift
armies, armies themselves. The ones carried
out by gangs in inner cities, the ones
done by crazy husbands in suburbs
or crazy cops on a power trip.
The one that has the most impact
right next door, made the local
paper. The one even mentioned in church
with much consternation and so little
instruction how to prevent it,
that it reminds you of the day they told
you Cain got Abel and you wanted to know
how Adam and Eve dealt with that.
The day they told you it was about
jealousy and anger—so you pretty
much figured it out over the years.
The day they told you Cain was given a mark;
and on some days,
in the right light,
you can almost see it
in the mirror.

Esperanza

"No one stays under," was the response
in Chile when thirty-three miners were trapped
in 2010. Although the Chilean President
did not know for sure if it would be
only bodies recovered—no one stays under!

The men set the Guinness World Record
for time underground—sixty-nine days.
They survived by eating one cracker apiece
every forty-eight hours, with some tuna
or mackerel on top—reminiscent of
the multiplication of the loaves and fishes
only this time by division. "We are
going to get out of here with God's help,"
one of them stated and then the men had to
wait and see just how God responds
in such situations when so many prayers
are sent His way. The same God
who once put writing on a wall
that none could decipher, save Daniel,
who translated the message for those assembled:

      1. Your days are numbered.

      2. You have been found wanting.

      3. Your kingdom will be divided.

When the final drill had pushed through
leaving its scoring on the side of the mineshaft
they lowered the Phoenix rescue pod. Over
a billion people viewed the rescue, ten times
the most-watched Super Bowl. One
of the miners was an expectant father. He
and his wife had chosen the name Carolina.
But the baby was re-named Esperanza.

The final detail was to make sure
all the miners had sunglasses so that
their retinas could be protected, so that they
could be delivered from darkness, like Esperanza
herself, baptized with ordinary light.

Entering Chappaquiddick

It's a difficult journey,
the road narrow, visibility limited
at times, especially in the darkness
when your memory of home
has something to do with getting there
but isn't going to save you
from every narrow bridge life gives you.
And we all have different vehicles,
with different abilities, different agilities,
and different life-expectancies.
Even a good driver can't see
every bad curve in the road,
expertly handle all road conditions
that come their way, account for every
other traveler using the same arteries.
We're all entering Chappaquiddick,
we're all under the influence of something
that keeps us from saying no to mortality.
We're all angels who decided to take a spin.
We all get into the passenger seat
when the trusted One opens the door
and offers us a ride.

Pigeonhole

(In every religion there is love, yet love has no religion. —Rumi)

I look at the *New York Times*
after the Paris shooting, the cover photo
with bullet holes through the exterior glass
of the restaurant, the untouched wine
glasses on the table behind, and marvel
how such enormous hate moves through
such tiny holes. For some reason
I think of the word pigeonhole and Google
the definition: Noun—a small compartment
for a domestic pigeon to nest. Verb—
deposit a document into a pigeonhole.
And I realize the document they are trying
to deposit through those holes is the Holy Quran.
Despite the fact that Muslim scholars released
an open letter to the Islamic State
in September meticulously blasting its ideology
and denouncing them as un-Islamic specifically
stating: "It is forbidden in Islam to torture...
it is forbidden in Islam to attribute evil
to God... It is forbidden in Islam to kill
the innocent... Jihad in Islam is defensive
war... It is forbidden in Islam to deny
women their rights... It is forbidden in Islam
to harm or mistreat—in any way—
Christians or any people of the Scripture."

The Irish musician, singer, songwriter,
Van Morrison, had a record titled:
"No Guru, No Method, No Teacher"
and the album sneered at critics who tried
to pigeonhole his religious beliefs while
he went on to write hit after hit
exploring the links between spirituality

and romantic love. He crooned, "Have I
told you lately that I love you?" And left
the listener deliciously choosing (like the Persian
poet Rumi) whether the Beloved referred-
to is with a small b or capital B.
Birds are meant to fly into the borderless
expansive sky, sail into the mystic
Van Morrison might say, but many prefer
to stay in a cage, force themselves through
pigeonholes into a tiny but safe
birdhouse; so tiny, so safe that only one
birdsong can echo off its walls.

The First Channel

(following an evening with a medium)

We miscommunicate—
you veiled in mystery,
me, descendant of Thomas.
Fill me with the spirit of Mercury,
send me a quicksilver messenger,
a miracle, a revelation!
Or support my childhood:
God-Man, Virgin Birth,
Immaculate Conception, the Trinity.
Give me an ism I can believe in—
give me atheism.
Remove the gods from the mountains
and rivers, from the trees
and animals. Make me an illiterate
to the Sacred Manuscript of Nature.
Give me newspaper horoscopes,
predict my future,
tell me of past lives,
give me stars, crosses, globes and mandalas
but don't tell me I'm a being of joy,
I don't want the responsibility;
and don't tell me that I'm perfect,
so that in the end
you're nothing but a radical,
and me, a heretic.

All Knowledge in Her Presence Falls Degraded

(from Milton's Paradise Lost *and the* Gnostic Gospels*)*

I always felt that the earth was my mother,
though I knew not of motherhood.
I would sit in the trees at cliff's edge
and watch the sun set, the moon rise,
marvel at the moving stars in the sky
and ponder my place in all of it, long before
I knew of years and months and days.
At night I would rest my head on the ground,
grasp the rich earth and ask for revelation.

You were sent as an instructor
to raise up me in whom there was no soul.
I remember your voice: "Adam, rise up!"
I rose and opened my eyes and cried
and we wondered what tears could be; but,
oh, the joy in seeing one's likeness.

Our favorite spot was near the tree of life,
its leaves like that of cypress,
stirring above us as we lay on the ground,
its clusters resembling white grapes,
ripening high in the heavens. And at its side,
the tree of knowledge with its magnificent dates.
Day upon day we passed talking beneath
grapevine, fig or pomegranate, thinking
that we were alone. But we were not alone.

Seven archangels came to us and said:
"Don't eat from the tree of knowledge..."
But the one who was called "the beast" came
and said: "... you will become like god..."
You took the fruit, gave it to me

and the light of knowledge shone for us.
And we put on shame seeing how naked
we were with regard to knowledge.

When we sobered we saw that we were naked
and became enamored of one another.
You touched me and I rose to meet you,
all being new and wonderful and fearful.
Your tears of blood puzzled us as the clear tears
from my eyes had confused us at our first meeting.
And we became one, though ashamed.

For our transgression of the commandment,
there came a great quaking in Paradise.
We fled from the searing heat of the surge,
hot ash finding us under the trees.
We ran through the fiery fields and looked
back through the quivering air and beheld
the rise and fall of the magma.

It was in the evening when we saw the Phoenix
come out of Paradise. Its shadow
passed over us three times, as the crocodiles
bore witness to our first baptism
with earthly water. Strangely,
I remember the olive tree, sprouted
among the thorns and bramble, whose oil
we would later use to anoint our sons.

Your belly swelled heavy with Cain
and you grew tired, needing sleep
and shelter and food. Many crafts I learned
to comfort you against the cold: weaponry
the first task—for the beasts turned against us.

I remember resting our hands on you to feel
Cain push and kick, not knowing, really,

that it was Cain but knowing that it was alive.
But you were fearful of what it might be
and wondered if it were punishment
for eating of the forbidden tree.

You cried in my arms your night of pain
and asked me if I thought you vile, loathsome.
I, the ignorant father, comforted you
and told you of my love and kissed your face
and pledged that I would rather be thrown
into the abyss of hell with you
than to return alone to Paradise.
And surprised even myself with that
spontaneity. Men are stupid that way.

A Type of Marriage

Carpe diem means seize the day,
but we rarely do. It's funny how
the rosebud poem is titled "To the Virgins,
to Make Much of Time." I knew a virgin
who went off to war in Vietnam.
He was a great warrior with an equally
great heart, and great, great, integrity.
He fell in love with a local girl and she
loved him but they never touched—
not one kiss. They didn't even
hold hands. I'm not making this up—
we sat together, two combat veterans,
two cancer patients sharing intimate
things. He hadn't seen her for over forty
years. She was a married woman. He
a married man—both in long-term
relationships. She was in stage four
breast cancer and arranged a trip
presumably to see her sister, but
the sister, who only lived an hour
from my veteran, colluded in the rendezvous.
He had given a ring at the end of his tour,
before returning to the States. Their meeting
was chaperoned by the sister, but they finally
got to touch—they hugged. He wanted me
to know two things. He said when they
embraced it was as if electric current
ran through his body. His eyes filled
with tears as he said, "Steve, I can only tell you—
it was magic!" The second thing he shared
was a card she sent when she returned home,
now, Paris, France. It was a short note.
It was overly polite. She said that it
was good to see him after so many years.
She said she was glad she made the trip against
doctor's orders, and her closing was: "Did you
notice on which finger I wore your ring?"
Carpe diem, my friends.

A Woman's Touch

In Andrew Wyeth's painting, Christina sits
on the wild grass, hundreds of yards
from the farmhouse, the barn, the buildings
constructed by men. She seems conflicted
whether to crawl up the hill to be
a part of all those obligations,
of housekeeping and homemaking, or
to stay grounded beyond the mowed fields
cut down to a manageable size
advertising the word: property.

The structures at the top of the hill
appear cold and empty. We feel
what is missing—it's been given a name.
And we know what Christina's going to do
after she inhales enough fragrance from the meadow.

She will drag herself up that hill
to the life she knows, take whatever
apple's within reach, bake it into
a pie, or feed it to a baby as apple-
sauce, repeat for the fifty billionth time
Eve's so necessary act—
so that men can label it temptation,
use it as a logo on a computer
to symbolize the bite they must take
from her hand in order to graduate
from ignorance.

The Shaker at Hancock House

I saw her huddled at the window
lost in reverie
and I imagined her recalling
Mother Ann's words
or simply the narrow beds,
the cupboards of butternut and pine
where, in her cotton gown and stockings,
she splashed cool water
from the washstand.
Perhaps it was winter,
another winter,
when she crouched by the wood-burning stove
in the yellow kitchen light
hearing the Elders and Eldresses,
Sisters and Brethren
following the scent of coffee
to wheat bread and milk,
butter and jam,
fried meat and applesauce.
Those spinners, weavers,
cooks, physicians,
and farmers.
Your hands to work...
Work
and Sabbath dancing
whirling, whirling in ecstasy.
...and your hearts to God...
...hearts to God
and a blessing will attend you.
But no—on second glance
I think she stared
at the once fertile fields,
long celibate
and gone to frost.

Snowflake or Bone

(the smallest of three California gray whales trapped in the
Beaufort Sea ice pack)

He imagines his chainsaw's constant
high-pitched ring filtering down
through the icy sea like sunlight,
her great body circling below
as intimate now with the percussion
of the pickaxe as a fetus
to the murmur of its mother's heart.

He stoops to tighten a mukluk lace,
examining the bloody ice where she
has chiseled her snout down to bone
against two narrowing windows of sky.

Another whaler suggests that they
put an end to the misery. He
half listens, recalling his first fish
floundering in the stern, his father's
hand firm around squirming silver, his
boyish heart pounding till the fish head
rinsed over the crimson deck.

Tonight, new chain arrives from Seattle
but the yearling no longer comes for air.
A transistor blares in the distance:
"Whales possess the earth's largest brain."
The sun flares, algae photosynthesize,
plankton feed, bottom-fish swallow,
whales consume. Snowflakes drift

over the closing squares, catch
in the wolverine hair of his parka,
melt into weathered crow's feet burning
at a glorious ninety-eight-point-six.

He strikes a match to a Marlboro,
the flame fighting, then snuffed in the wind,
the charred match head blown like a tiny bone
onto the blue ice. He strikes a second,
the light as alive in his black eyes
as a boyhood memory,
as the spirit of the whale upon the wind,
no longer matter, but fact.

Amnesia

(thoughts sparked by the Allman Brothers' Live at the Fillmore*)*

It's amazing how many people believe in angels,
heavenly beings of all kind, as well as
magical earthly creatures—leprechauns,
mermaids, fairies, pixies, or those hovering
in between like ghosts or jinn. They want
to embrace science, but science tells you that
you're worm food, dust that just becomes
dust; and we all have too high an opinion
of ourselves to think of our ashes, our final
resting place, synonymous with the bag
we empty from the vacuum cleaner. No,
we have what I call the hunch—that
the creation story is based on some form
of reality, provable or not, where
the dust was scooped up, breathed into
and animated with something like a soul.
Soul! There's an interesting word—
what the hell does *that* word mean?
Einstein said: "Energy cannot be created
or destroyed," giving us at least one
scientist who said we were eternal.
And even if it's obvious that the body
ages, dies, decays, we wonder about
that energy, those brainwaves, those thoughts,
or consciousness living on somewhere—
reminiscent of the day they told you astronomers
viewing supernovas are really witnessing
suns exploded centuries ago but it takes
that long for particles (or is it waves?) of
light to reach the observer. And the mind starts
to ponder whether the solar body died
then or now—or whether it still hasn't died
for the alien in a "galaxy far, far away."

And how, under that formula, it *is* eternal—
the light continuing to travel through darkness;
the illusion being the resting place, the lay-by,
the scenic overlook that never was your home.
But, as the Adam and Eve story suggests:
more like a penance, more like a forced amnesia
concerning Paradise, more like the Chosen
People temporarily enslaved—the one time
you forgot you had celestial wings because
you were tied to the whipping post.

Onward Faithful Soldiers

"Young Man in Suit at Door" was a poem I wrote
about youthful enthusiasm for proselytizing.
Now it is thirty years later and two witnesses
show up at my door wanting to discuss
the Book of Revelations—their hearts still
in afterglow from the seduction of God—
not a lover-God who holds you
in conjugal embrace, but a father-God
reinforcing family first, the tribe.

I'm not put off by their affirmations
as I once was by the twenty-one-year-old
"elder" who had so much to teach me.
This couple is twice his age. They show me
scripture; they are desperate to share with the world.
I want to embrace them. I resist the temptation
to say someone sits on a mountaintop
in the Black Hills or the Himalayas
wanting to share their own exquisite heartthrob.
I know they will knock on many doors this beautiful
morning. I know they will have many doors shut
in their face. I want to tell them what I've learned
from studying scripture, that there is more than one
result that can come from such excavation,
that even prayer can become a ditch that we keep
digging and digging so that only a Samaritan
would have any interest in saving us now.

Don't Refuse the Call

One Puff of a Smoke Signal

Jesus, Jesus, Jesus, Jesus,
Buddha, Buddha, Buddha, Buddha,
Yahweh, Yahweh, Yahweh, Yahweh,
Allah, Allah, Allah, Allah,
Shiva, Shiva, Shiva, Shiva,
D,D,D,D,
G,G,G,G,
A,A,A,A;
I push the zebra keys of the piano
one at a time, again and again.
I push the foot pedals to adjust volume,
F,F,F,F,
B,B,B,B,
I close my eyes.
Black Elk walks through the room,
pauses, smiles at me, speaks:
"Learn the chords, Steve,
learn an introduction,
listen to another instrument,
there is more than one beat to a drum,
one puff of a smoke signal
says nothing."

Enlightenment

I feel a kindred spirit in Joseph Campbell and his *Power of Myth*—
an ex-Catholic who discovered God really was everywhere, and
spoke more languages than you ever gave Him credit for. He was
even transgender from time-to-time, depending on the needs of
His people—you know the ones he made in His image and after
His likeness? Male and female He created them in His image and
after His likeness. Yes, I know I'm repeating myself—I do that
whenever there's an important item on the shopping list. Most
people, like my father, are born into and stay in the same religion
for their entire life. He never went shopping for other answers.
He was a good man, the best; but he also never went shopping
for an answer to how a country of Christians threw six million
Jews into ovens.

Lately I've been looking into Shamanism, becoming open to
ever-new possibilities. With cancer you question everything in life
you thought was certain. I watch the constellations in the heavens—
I don't see any fixed stars. Every day they are in a new location. I
watch people go in and out of places of worship. I admire their
devotion to certain prayers, certain chants, certain creeds. I no
longer have time to wait on enlightenment like a college degree
earned through arduous study. I am only interested in the mail-in
matchbook diploma that takes no effort at all. I have been reduced
to two interests: laughter and love.

There is no amount of time that can save me.
There is no amount of soap that can wash my soul.
I no longer have patience for questions like:
"Do I circle the temple clockwise or counterclockwise?"

Death by Beetle

You told me about the whippoorwill
brought to the clinic, the surgery,
the beetles that went undigested
and I laughed at the bird who could not fly,
who tried to live upon the ground

and never thought of my brother,
back from war,
the heavy drinking, barroom brawls
and the ghosts who walked with him at night.

"Some things can't be digested,"
you said, "you have to go in, remove
the obstruction," and proceeded to tell me how
you sliced her open and plucked each beetle
one by one. Your whippoorwill,
exorcised and snug with silk,
began to sing again that day.

Once, on a visit, he and I
heard a whippoorwill cry across
the creek. My brother slipped from moonlight,
his hands claiming honed steel
from its hidden sheath. There
in the black wood I felt a chill,
familiar as my name,
something barely tamed
by water, barley, malt, hops and yeast.

Weightless

They had lived through the Depression and World War II
in order for their children to rock and roll.
They had seen hobos and dustbowls and labor riots,
the look of rage in the eyes of those who had nothing
left to lose, felt vulnerable with Pearl Harbor,
vindicated by Hiroshima, numbed by the details
of gas chambers and ovens and Bataan Death Marches,
wanted Levittowns and musicals, every humble dwelling
a mirror image of equality, every citizen singing in the rain,
every child protected, every soldier on a GI Bill
turning swords to ploughshares and Nobel Prizes.

They constructed superhighways and filling stations
so that we could reach out and touch one another,
cars with fins to enhance the illusion of speed;
hurl a metal object through the air that is not a rocket,
not related to Buzz Bombs or nuclear tests.

Eisenhower warned of a military-industrial complex,
but veterans were listening to Perry Como and Andy Williams
singing "Moon River" and everyone dreaming
of some Huckleberry friend. Sputnik broke that reverie
like an air raid siren over Honolulu. Kennedy said
we'd put a man on the moon and kids twisted and stomped
their way toward civil rights and "Make Love Not War,"
claiming this land was their land and the answers
were blowing in the winds of change. Americans could see
themselves sailing down the Mississippi on a raft
with Harry Belafonte or Sidney Poitier but not Malcolm or Martin.
Assassination re-introducing the sacrificial lambs of God
who are supposed to take away the sins of the world
through examination of hatred, culpability, the up-side
of guilt and shame—every one of us washing our hands
like Pilate, and Christ's kind words echoing down the centuries—
"Father forgive them for they know not what they do."

Neil Armstrong seemed to set us right when he said,
"... one giant leap for mankind." But you could almost hear
Abigail Adams saying, "Don't forget the ladies"
in those "All men are created equal" statements.
And for God's sake, stop planting real-estate flags!

There is a popular myth that the only man-made structure
that can be seen from outer space is the Great Wall of China—
and we are told it is a great wonder.
But Robert Frost told us eloquently,
"Something there is that doesn't love a wall."
Reagan said, "Mr. Gorbachev, tear down this wall."
And, as in Eve's delight, Gorbachev took a giant bite
from that apple and there was Glasnost, Perestroika,
Strategic Arms Reduction, the Gipper's Shining City
on the Hill—the dream of every religion—the land
of milk and honey, the city paved with streets of gold;
all those places of worship made with brick and mortar
and workers wanting to build walls to contain the good news.

Pope Francis said you must be more interested
in building bridges than walls
which is why Mark Twain said
travel is fatal to bigotry.
It is why a cosmonaut
hands a throat lozenge
to an astronaut
just because he heard a cough
echo in their place of worship—
two members of a cult—
two lucky ones who know what it is
to be truly weightless.

Eve

Over forty years I remembered her.
Two, no, three marriages had passed
through us like tides leaving their etchings;
and the things lifted by tides—
the children and grandchildren.
I was the schoolboy with the schoolboy crush
who drove 1,200 miles with grandfatherly stubble
to find the one who could have been my bride.
These things don't work out,
I'm sure, for the hordes carrying
youthful fantasies.
And it doesn't matter to me that it sounds like a lie
that her beauty had grown
but the face was the face I left behind
and the soul was that of Eve,
saying over and over, "Adam,
open your eyes."

Cure Is the Wrong Four-Letter Word

I will not be going to see the mummified head of Saint Catherine.
Nor will I go to Lourdes, Jerusalem or Bethlehem. Unless it is
Pennsylvania and I can find healing in a cup of coffee served
by a struggling waitress. I won't be traveling halfway round the
world seeking the miracle cure but I will see the local shaman,
consider the recommended acupuncture, take every suggestion
from family and friend at least semi-seriously—the green tea,
the ginseng, the ginger, the vitamin C and D; ingest only things
organic. I will remain polite to each helpful, loving gesture and
accept at least half of them as I walk the ridgepole between
herbalist and oncologist, healers with rosaries or white lab coats.
I want to welcome every good wish and blessing but I will not
be coerced or seduced by experimental treatments, statistics
translated as conventional wisdom, if it doesn't match my
version of common sense.

What I will do is take the supplements offered by my wife, feel
her fingertips in the palm of my hand, make eye contact with her
just before I swallow, remembering that moment before ingest-
ing the communion wafer (wars are fought over that moment—
the debate between miracle or placebo), fix my eyes on her so
that I can see the same light that lights the whole universe.

Tomb of the Unknown

There were a million musicians before Mary
Fahl, innumerable compositions on every
subject imaginable, including war,
including "Going Home." I wanted a piece
of music that I could play for my final salute
in uniform; a salute to my fallen comrades.

On YouTube I saw the flag-draped casket
so I clicked and twenty minutes later,
through all the tears I failed to shed in war,
the wound was opened and cleansed by her voice.

She, who'd never been to war or strapped
on battle rattle, helped remove my body-
armor so I could walk more freely
down the road that would take me home
to the hills, home to the graves, home
to the repository of music: the human heart.

Here's a toast to all the hearts that got
to sing again. And here's a toast to all
we put in tombs.

The Rising Tide of Hate

As if it just started!
As if Cain didn't terrorize Abel.
As if the whole world, save one
family in an ark, wasn't wiped out
because of displeasure. As if the Hebrew
Bible and the Quran don't tell
this story of Noah. As if the message didn't
go deep in the psyche, that God favors some
over others. As if everyone
has forgotten what God said to Noah
when He gave him the rainbow as a sign
of His covenant with earth for all generations
to come, quote: "And from each human being,
too, I will demand an accounting for
the life of another human being." Later
He had to put it in writing: "Thou shalt not kill."

All religions pay at least lip-service
to this commandment until they get scared,
and their bloodline to Cain starts to boil;
and the amnesia sets in about the lesson
that Abel, the peaceful one, was the one
who was pleasing to God. And the symbol God gave
to Noah that there would be, at last, an end
to the ordeal, was the olive branch
in the beak of the dove.

My wife, the professor, is dovish. She works
with people in conflict. They are drowning. She brings
them an olive branch. She swings out
of bed each morning, puts her feet
on the floor to measure the tide rising—
thankful to feel dry land.

The Medal for Finishing Last

They gave me a medal for finishing last.
Me who has a box full of harrier trophies
in the attic. Me who set the obstacle
course record at Officer Training School
in San Antonio, Texas. Me who ran
the Boston Marathon, jumped from helicopters,
in the mountains of Afghanistan, wearing
forty pounds of body armor. That's
how I tore the ACL; before the cancer,
before the labrums torn in both hips,
before the chemotherapy and the high-
dose steroids, before the meniscus tear
that ended the running and made me a walker—
walking with poets and eight-year-olds,
while the runners pull away, giving
me a glimpse of my past. And the other walkers
pass me, so that, like visiting
a nursing home, I get a peek at the future.

Jesus said the first shall be last,
the meek shall inherit the earth.
I'm getting meeker.
But I don't see the meek inheriting
anything. I see the ambitious sprinting
to the lead; to be number one,
cross the finish line spent and alone.
I take up the rear reluctantly.
I need to re-write my life story.
Maybe turn poet or cow-herder,
learn humility, how to lead from behind.

The Blessed Way

(Saint James Retreat Center, Tiverton, Rhode Island)

At Saint James tall grasses
flame-dance with ocean wind.
They whisper: "Fan your flames! Fan your flames!
Dance this oh-so-simple dance."
Let your light burn so brightly
you may have to set your tail-end
down in the cool bay,
like each duck who lands in the placid cove,
sending ripples rolling away
toward the craggy shore.
There pilgrims meditate
lovely as driftwood
docked where there is NO LIFEGUARD posted.

Up on the hill a white statue of Jesus
welcomes you with open arms,
His Sacred Heart bursting with glorious light
shooting compass rays in every direction.
But what ocean breeze
could fan a heart of stone
enough to light the whole universe?

Just this morning the sun rose
like a platinum host
over an emerald altar
rousing a choir of birdsong.
Waves were waking
all the shoreline stones with light.
Rocks began to swim
like fish boiling the shallows.
Bees were singing praises
to the sweet perfumed air of morn
and I could see the grasses through my window
move as one.
They were saying:
"Dance!"

So We Have Poetry

Even the dying can't make you listen
to what you don't know,
what you have no time to know,
what you don't need to know
to continue on your merry way,
or not so merry—downright miserable
at times. In fact, those are the times
you come the closest to listening
because you have to
in order to be rescued.
But even those times get busy
with talk or alcohol or some other
addiction to escaping reality—
the reality that you're a clock ticking
with moveable parts that are getting
worn by time even as we speak.
And every painstaking advance
of this stubborn species
practically goes unnoticed
by the slow tick of history—
so much so that although there is
barely a trace element in the DNA
of danger from the neighboring savage tribe
when you go to the waterhole,
there is the Nobel Prize winner
helping to split atoms
that could end all tribes,
poison all waterholes.
Marshall McLuhan said, "The medium is the message."
and the medium *is* the message
to the extent that reality TV stars
now run for office and you could bleed
to death from the thousand paper cuts
known as sound bites. News has become
entertainment; the macabre gaining in

popularity by networks competing in
rating wars, with the natural outcome
of celebrity trumping public service, public interest.
Even the dying can't make you listen
above that much noise pollution, news pollution,
to discover that Solomon was right after all,
there is nothing new under the sun,
and the Golden Rule, the one thing
that could save us all, sits on the bench
with the other substitutes, listening to the star
trash-talk. No, even the dying
can't make you listen to the only sounds
that have ever moved you—the lullaby,
the rock-and-roll that kick-started
your sex life and the hymn that suggested
that you were eternal. Even the dying
can't make you listen to the voices
of the dead, who are dying to be heard.
Yes, I mean that literally—
so we have poetry.

Base Camp

Leslie Binns abandoned his ascent of Mt. Everest
to save another climber. He was 500 meters
from the top of the world when he successfully
broke her fall, shared his oxygen, saved her
frostbitten hands. All his preparations, expenses,
traded for the experience of being more alive;
starting a new climb called descent—
a falling upward like three days in the tomb.

Sanita Hazra later said of her rescuer:
"God sent him to me." Funny the places
one encounters God—on the mountaintop,
in the tabernacle, on the battlefield,
at the end of a rope, in a classroom.

In Kathmandu, there is a belief that every guest
is a god. *Namaste* meaning: *When the god
in me greets the god in you we are one.*

We brave steep slopes hoping to stand
victorious at the summit, settle for base camps
where we share our gifts, rescued by
deities we meet along the way.

Sixty Candles

(NJ DeVico's birthday)

They said it was your last birthday.

The rest of us pretend
we can imagine what that's like:
to be addicted to light and color;
and your dealer, no, not even the dealer,
but some kid on the corner
peddling for the dealer,
tells you no more sales, no more highs,
and the addiction was so comfortable
it had spread to the lows,
so that even sorrow, even depression,
had become damaged friends.

The forest, the sounds of bees and birdsong,
the one canvas you liked already painted,
and not abstract to the ordinary eye,
but filled with an abundance of realism.

Now comes the big question—
where does realism get you?
You look at the rabbit covered with flies
and say, "That's where, stupid!"
But then you find the fledgling
hopping in the underbrush,
the mother squawking anxiously.

"Why should I care?" You ask yourself,
why should anyone care...

... care enough to buy you a cake,
adorn it with candles;
so many little points of light

and the off-key singing of loved ones—
like hands cupped around your body,
and, even against your will,
lifting you into the nest.

Don't Refuse the Call

(for my wife)

Don't refuse the call!

When a powerful stranger knocks on the door
don't think it is a prophet dressed in fine clothes.
Sometimes the beggar at the door in rags,
the leper at the door in pain,
do not want entry.
Sometimes you stand on the threshold together
and suddenly see the walls that held you in,
suddenly hear more clearly the birdsong
outside praising dawn.

With the birth of that light
we have constructed clocks,
the gift timed in seconds, minutes, days and years.
We have constructed cities and towers
both outside and within ourselves—
so many stairways to heaven that have become Babel,
that perpetuate the Great Diaspora.

Now that we can hear the tapping sound on the door
take my hand and let us open it together.

Acknowledgments

Passages North: "Snowflake or Bone," "The Shaker at Hancock House"

U.S. 1 Worksheets: "The Orchestration of War," "Still Life"

National Public Radio (Morning Edition): "Let the Children Come to Me," "Old Farts in A Young War," "High Grounds"

Schuylkill Valley Journal: "I'm Leaning toward the Milky Way," "The Blessed Way"

River Heron Review: "A Woman's Touch," "Last Night at the Widow's Poetry Reading on Martha's Vineyard"

Journal of Military Experience and the Arts: "Band of Brothers"

The Devil's Millhopper: "Death by Beetle"

About the Author

Steve Nolan did his undergraduate work at the University of Miami in English and Psychology and his masters at Barry University, in clinical social work, also in Miami, Florida. He is a Licensed Clinical Social Worker who spent 25 years as a therapist and 30 years in the military ending his career as the Chief of Combat Stress for Paktika Province in Afghanistan. He ran a PTSD clinic for the VA for five years before moving to Newtown, Pennsylvania, in 2015.

His work has been published in: *Passages North, U.S. 1 Worksheets, Florida Review, Woodrider, Devil's Millhopper Press, Gypsy (Amnesty International Edition), Schuylkill Valley Journal* and others. His poems were featured on Morning Edition, National Public Radio, September 24, 2007, upon his return from Afghanistan in a story called, "Mother, Son Share Experiences of War." He is the author of *Go Deep*, a collaboration with the artist NJ DeVico.

CPSIA information can be obtained
at www.ICGtesting.com
Printed in the USA
BVHW031314291219
568011BV00002B/26/P